inSiDE ouT

BAD GIRL

I CAN'T HANDLE MY MIND. ITS TOR

WANT THE SOUL STRIPPER "GO SHAW
BAD GIRL. PEOPLE ARE STARVING or PUNISH YOUR SE
SELF-CENTERED, GREEDY, LAZY, MY GIRL" ATTABE
MOTHER, STOMPING ON THE ME WITH BIG BLACK BOOT
KILL MEW NOW! I CAN'T MAKE IT HERE, I WON'T

inside out

PORTRAIT OF AN EATING DISORDER written and illustrated by nadia shivack

ginee seo books
Atheneum Books for Young Readers
New York London Toronto Sydney

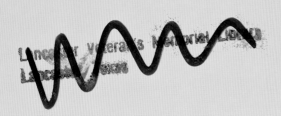

Atheneum Books for Young Readers
An imprint of Simon & Schuster's Children's Publishing Division
1230 Avenue of the Americas
New York, New York 10020

Book design by Polly Kanevsky
The text for this book is set in Dana and EC Franklin Gothic.
The illustrations for this book are rendered in ink, crayon, and colored pencil.
Manufactured in China

First Edition
10 9 8 7 6 5 4 3 2 1

Library of Congress Cataloging-in-Publication Data
Shivak, Nadia.
Inside out: portrait of an eating disorder/written and illustrated by Nadia Shivack.—1st ed.
p.   cm.
"Ginee Seo Books."
ISBN-13: 978-0-689-85216-9
ISBN-10: 0-689-85216-9
[1. Shivack, Nadia—Health. 2. Bulimia—Patients—United States—Biography.]
I. Title.
RC552.B84S495 2005
616.85'263'0092—dc22   2004016096

TO ALL THOSE BEFORE ME
WHO HAVE PAVED THE WAY
AND HAVE ENSURED THAT
THIS AND OTHER ILLNESSES
ARE NOT HIDDEN AWAY.

DAY BY DAY, MEAL BY MEAL,
MILLIONS OF GIRLS AND WOMEN
IN THE UNITED STATES
STRUGGLE WITH EATING DISORDERS.

I AM ONE OF THEM.

I FIRST BECAME AWARE OF FOOD
WHEN I WAS SIX YEARS OLD. I WOULD HOARD
CANDY IN MY SOCK DRAWER. I ONLY SHOWED
SPECIAL PEOPLE MY HIDDEN TREASURE.

I NEVER TOUCHED ANY OF IT. IT WAS SACRED.

MY MOTHER HAD SURVIVED THE HOLOCAUST, WHICH SHE REFUSED TO TALK ABOUT. BECAUSE OF IT, SHE HAD VERY STRONG IDEAS ABOUT FOOD. WE COULDN'T GO TO BED UNTIL WE HAD FINISHED EVERYTHING ON OUR PLATES.

+ FEAR (FOR ALL)!

I wish they'd all stop fighting and mom would eat and little sis stop wheezing and I can't stand all this noise!

I wish I could disappear. I wish little sis would go away and big sis SHUT UP!

AT THE SAME TIME, MY MOTHER ALLOWED HERSELF ONLY ONE MEAL A DAY—USUALLY LATE AT NIGHT. SHE ATE JUST ENOUGH TO KEEP HERSELF GOING, NOT A BITE MORE.

FORTY-TWO PERCENT OF STUDENTS BETWEEN THE FIRST AND THIRD GRADES WANT TO BE THINNER.

WHEN I WAS TWELVE, MY BEST FRIEND WAS A GIRL NAMED AMY. SHE WAS ALWAYS ON A DIET. SHE WOULD GO TO WEIGHT WATCHERS MEETINGS WITH HER MOM.

EIGHTY PERCENT OF WOMEN ARE DISSATISFIED WITH THEIR APPEARANCE.

FORTY-FIVE PERCENT OF WOMEN ARE ON A DIET ON ANY GIVEN DAY.

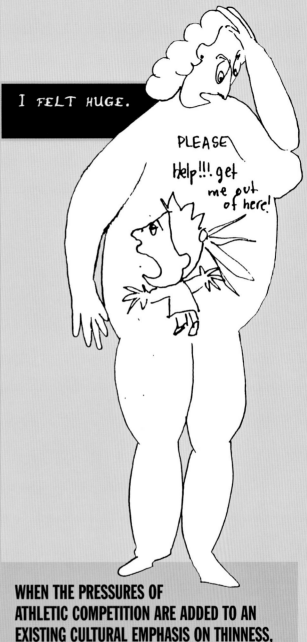

WHEN THE PRESSURES OF ATHLETIC COMPETITION ARE ADDED TO AN EXISTING CULTURAL EMPHASIS ON THINNESS, THE RISKS INCREASE FOR ATHLETES TO DEVELOP DISORDERED EATING.

gosh, I'm so so hungry from skipping dinner; their lunches look so good! **How** do they eat without getting fat? I don't know what to do. I feel so alone. I wish I could eat just a **"FEW"** fries. What's wrong with me?

Brrr, it's cold!! Why'd I eat all those cookies last night when I told Dad I wouldn't? Why can't I be good + have willpower? I'll have to make up for the calories by walking all the way downtown and back. I'll lie to mom. I'll tell her I'm eating at Mel's and skip dinner. I'll **HAVE** to start a new diet tomorrow!!

While Nad walks and **walks** and **walks**, the same endlessss thoughts **SWIRL** like snow **around** and around in her head

I THOUGHT ABOUT FOOD CONSTANTLY.

MY SWIMMING AND SCHOOLWORK BEGAN TO SUFFER. MORE AND MORE, I COULD ONLY THINK ABOUT DIETS AND WEIGHT LOSS.

THE DIETS BECAME MORE EXTREME. SO DID THE BINGES, WHICH WERE SO LARGE THAT I WAS IN SEVERE PAIN AFTER EATING. I BEGAN TO EXPERIMENT WITH PURGING. I BOUGHT MEDICINES LIKE IPECAC TO HELP ME THROW UP UNTIL I GOT BETTER AT DOING IT ON MY OWN.

BEDTIME! (attempting to sleep with little sister wheezing—very scary)

DINNER!! (filled with tension, fighting, anxiety... oh, and food too)

FRIENDS! (try so hard to be popular/cool)

I TRIED TO EAT NORMALLY, BUT I COULDN'T.

IT WAS AS IF AN ALIEN FORCE INSIDE ME DROVE ME ON.

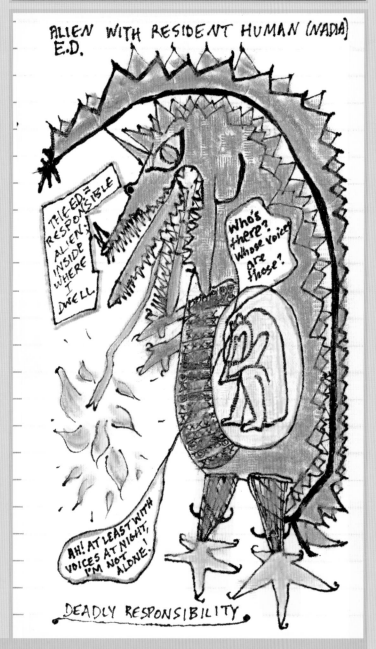

I awaken ◉ eat breakfast ◉ eat lunch ◉ **try to** make it through

With each meal, the tension, anxiety and feeling of "size" grows inside me! **No matter how hard I try,** I end the day with a binge and purge for **relief** and to "**shrink**" back down to size. Everything about me is "small" now except for the shame and despair. And so goes the cycle **ON** and **ON** and **ON!**

dinner; after the **Binge** and **Purge**

BY THE TIME I WAS FOURTEEN, I HAD FOUND MY ROUTINE. I ATE BREAKFAST, LUNCH, AND EVEN MADE IT THROUGH DINNER. BUT EACH EVENING I BROKE DOWN AND ATE CRAZILY, AT A HUNDRED MILES PER HOUR—AND THEN MADE MYSELF VOMIT.

AFTER THE FRENZY OF THE BINGE AND PURGE, I FELT RELIEVED—NUMB, CALM, DISASSOCIATED FROM MY BODY AND THE WORLD. ALMOST IMMEDIATELY, THOUGH, I FELT ASHAMED AND GUILTY. I HATED MYSELF.

THE CYCLE TOOK ON A LIFE OF ITS OWN. SOON I HARDLY ATE BREAKFAST OR LUNCH. I WATCHED AS OTHER KIDS ATE ALL MY FORBIDDEN FOODS.

FORBIDDEN FOODS:
HERO, FRENCH FRIES, BREAD, HAMBURGERS, HOT DOGS, POTATO CHIPS, PRETZELS, SODA, CANDY, ICE CREAM, SANDWICHES, PIZZA, PASTA—EVEN YOGURT!

GOOD FOODS:
FRUIT, VEGETABLES, COFFEE (TWELVE CUPS A DAY)

ONE-THIRD OF INDIVIDUALS WHO SUFFER FROM EATING DISORDERS REPORT THAT THE ONSET OF THEIR ILLNESS OCCURRED BETWEEN THE AGES OF ELEVEN AND FIFTEEN.

I SOCIALIZED LESS AND LESS. I FORGOT HOW TO LAUGH.

MY THROAT HURT ALL THE TIME. THE GLANDS UNDER MY CHIN SWELLED UP FROM ALL THE VOMITING.

EATING DISORDERS ARE NOT DUE TO A FAILURE OF WILL OR BEHAVIOR. THEY ARE REAL, TREATABLE MEDICAL ILLNESSES IN WHICH CERTAIN PATTERNS OF EATING TAKE ON A LIFE OF THEIR OWN.

THIS IS WHAT HAPPENS WHEN YOU PURGE.

SIDE EFFECTS
FROM PURGING INCLUDE:
RUPTURE OF ESOPHAGUS
TOOTH DECAY
DEHYDRATION
ELECTROLYTE IMBALANCES
IRREGULAR HEARTBEATS
POSSIBLE HEART FAILURE . . .
AND DEATH

The eating disorder took over my life. I quit swimming. I was too weak and shaky to compete. But it never occurred to me that I was sick.

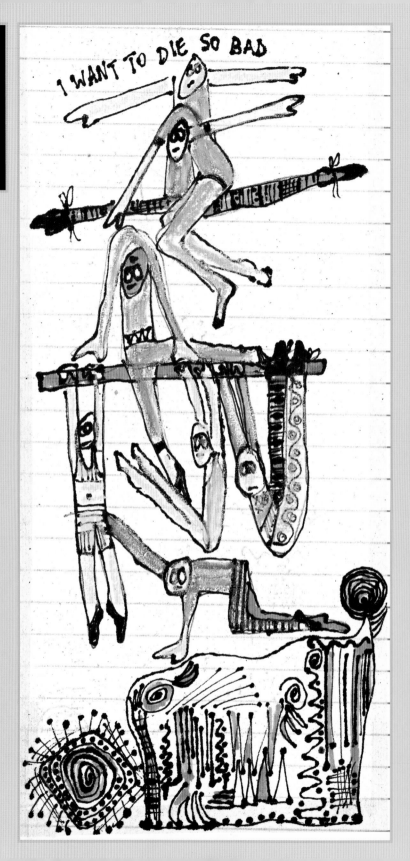

THE SUMMER I WAS SIXTEEN, I DECIDED TO GO TO CALIFORNIA WITH MY BEST FRIEND FROM HIGH SCHOOL. I'D SAVED SOME MONEY FROM BABYSITTING AND TEACHING SWIMMING CLASSES. MY PARENTS WERE SEPARATING, AND OUR HOME LIFE WAS PAINFUL. I NEEDED TO GET AWAY.

MY FRIEND AND I STAYED WITH HER FATHER'S NEW FAMILY FOR THREE DAYS IN L.A. IT WAS A DISASTER. HER FAMILY WAS ALSO GOING THROUGH A BAD TIME. THE WHOLE TIME THERE, I BINGED AND PURGED LIKE CRAZY, IN SECRET.

BULIMIA NERVOSA IS FREQUENTLY ASSOCIATED WITH SYMPTOMS OF DEPRESSION AND CHANGES IN SOCIAL ADJUSTMENT.

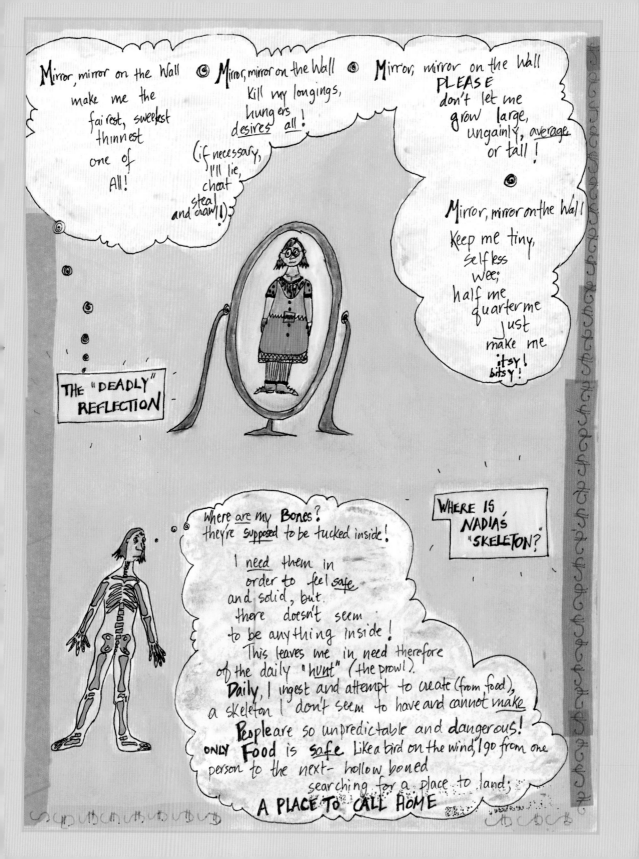

I WAS LOSING CONTROL. I WAS TERRIFIED. I DIDN'T KNOW WHAT TO DO OR WHERE TO GO, BUT I KNEW I COULDN'T STAY WITH MY FRIEND. I FOUND A HOTEL IN L.A. THAT ALLOWED ME TO PAY FOR ONE MONTH'S STAY. I NEVER LEFT MY ROOM EXCEPT LATE AT NIGHT TO GET FOOD. THE REST OF THE TIME I SLEPT.

I GAINED A LOT OF WEIGHT.

I LEFT THAT HOTEL AND FOUND A PLACE IN SAN FRANCISCO, WHERE I SPENT THE REST OF THE SUMMER SLEEPING, EATING, AND VOMITING.

MANY PEOPLE STRUGGLING WITH BULIMIA NERVOSA RECOGNIZE THAT THEIR BEHAVIORS ARE UNUSUAL, EVEN DANGEROUS.

NINETEEN PERCENT OR MORE OF COLLEGE-AGE WOMEN IN AMERICA ARE BULIMIC.

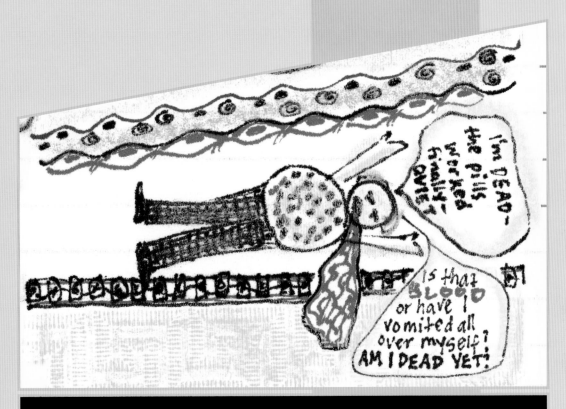

I WAS IN A KIND OF TRANCE.

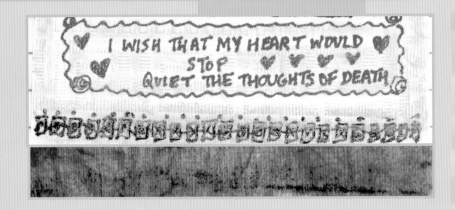

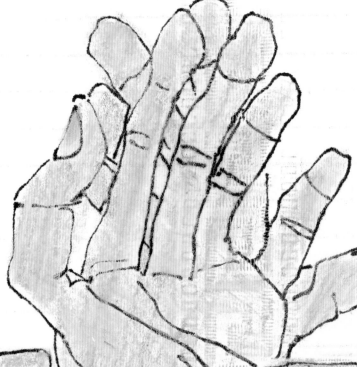

"THIS TOO SHALL PASS"

UNDERNEATH THIS HAND
LAYS ANOTHER
TO CATCH THE FALL
INTO MENTAL ILLNESS

I CAN CHOOSE ALTERNATIVES TO THE E.D. ART &

I NEEDNT GIVE THE ED THE POWER/ CONTROL TO TAKE OVER ME LIFE

my ® hand beneath my Ⓛ hand

THIS IS ME CHOOSING TO HOLD MYSELF UP- THE PART OF ME THAT GROWS WEAK + DESPAIRING. THE ® HAND WILL CATCH ME, HELP ME TO MAKE THE RIGHT CHOICE

SLOWLY I BEGAN TO FEEL BETTER AND SLEEP LESS. IT WAS TIME TO GO BACK TO NEW YORK, TO PULL MY LIFE TOGETHER. I DECIDED TO SKIP MY SENIOR YEAR OF HIGH SCHOOL AND TAKE AN EARLY ADMISSION TO CITY COLLEGE. I WANTED TO MOVE OUT OF MY PARENTS' APARTMENT AND LIVE ON MY OWN.

I FOUND A TINY PLACE IN MANHATTAN. BUT IN THE ISOLATION OF MY HOME, THE BINGING AND PURGING BEGAN ONCE MORE. IT BEGAN TO FEEL LIKE A REWARD, EVEN A COMFORT. IT WAS HOW I COPED WITH MY LONELINESS, MY SADNESS, MY FEARS, AND MY HAPPINESS.

THE SOONER EATING DISORDERS ARE DIAGNOSED AND TREATED, THE BETTER THE OUTCOMES ARE LIKELY TO BE.

I STARTED WORKING AT A DELI AND ATTENDING CLASSES. I WANTED TO BE A DOCTOR, LIKE MY DAD. BUT BIT BY BIT I GAVE UP ON THINGS I LOVED. I QUIT GUITAR, READING, WRITING, AND TEAM SPORTS, SO I COULD SPEND MORE TIME BY MYSELF.

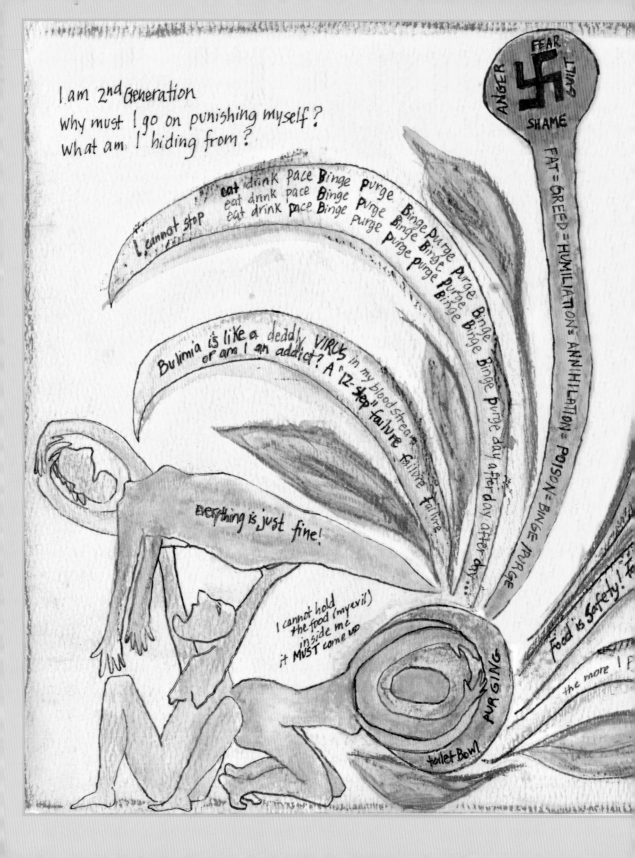

The **lilac** is the emblem of the forsaken

I am as a concentration camp victim, denied permission to enjoy life, I must grow lean hard ready

...s Home, Food is Always there to hold me tight in this dangerous mind + life!

you don't deserve to eat you greedy greedy pig!

"isn't she disgusting always trying to get attention manipulate + charm give gifts, make them love her."

"yeah, such a brown nose always trying to be miss goody goody impress everyone, thinks she knows everything what an asshole."

...e the more I become like a stone away from people + myself

I FOUND A WAY TO ALWAYS BE NEAR FOOD. INSTEAD OF STUDYING, I'D SPEND TIME DECIDING WHAT FOODS I'D EAT AND THROW UP THAT NIGHT. FOOD WAS MY DRUG.

I STOPPED GETTING MY PERIOD.

IT TOOK ME SEVEN AND A HALF YEARS TO GRADUATE FROM COLLEGE. I JUST COULDN'T CONCENTRATE. MY LIFE REVOLVED AROUND MY NIGHTLY EATING RITUALS, WHEN I MIGHT BINGE SIX OR SEVEN TIMES IN THE COURSE OF AN EVENING.

ONLY A SMALL NUMBER OF SCHOOLS AND COLLEGES HAVE PROGRAMS TO EDUCATE YOUNG PEOPLE ABOUT THE DANGERS OF EATING DISORDERS.

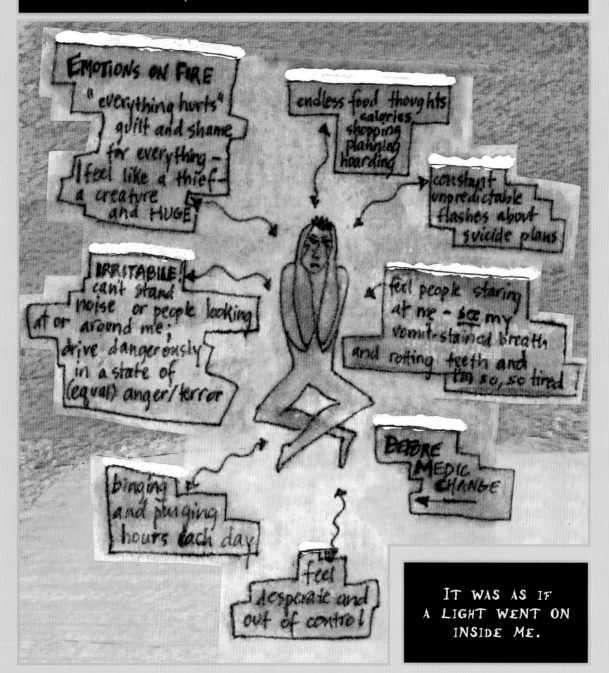

IT WAS AS IF A LIGHT WENT ON INSIDE ME.

↓AFTER

with her new "coat" on to cover the raw emotions, nerve endings; shielding Had from the onslaught of noise, thoughts, and shame. She has a warm, gentle padding over her own "fire" and life is once more MANAGEABLE!

My BINGES DROPPED TO ONCE OR TWICE A NIGHT.

SOME MEDICATIONS, PRIMARILY ANTIDEPRESSANTS, HAVE BEEN FOUND HELPFUL FOR PEOPLE WITH BULIMIA, PARTICULARLY THOSE WITH SIGNIFICANT SYMPTOMS OF DEPRESSION OR ANXIETY.

BUT I WASN'T CURED. MEDICATIONS COULD ONLY DO SO MUCH. I WAS STILL OBSESSED WITH FOOD, AND SOON I WAS BACK TO BINGEING AND VOMITING WHENEVER I COULD.

DOWN! GRRR!OBEY! OR DIE!

Bulimia Monster (what else could it be? who makes me binge and purge over and over and over and over and over.

WHY CAN'T I STOP? I am so weak -willed - addicted

I TRIED TO FIND SOMETHING THAT COULD SAVE ME— TO KEEP THE ALIEN INSIDE ME FROM COMING OUT AT NIGHT.

Sun 2⁰⁰pm coffee shop

DEAR♡
    I am so angry and disappointed in myself - I haven't been able to "fight off" a binge + purge for the past 5 nites. I have painted from dawn to dusk, made countless necklaces + earrings (for Jude's B'day) + worked out. I don't even seem to want to fight...it is so much easier this way though I hate myself all the more. Again down on hands + knees before the "monster," (MY BULIMIA MONSTER). I tell myself to try and live as much as I can ~~live~~, between the binges and purges,+ shame and fear of being "found out". At this ~~x~~ level, maintaining DIGNITY is not easy Dear♡. Only you know how little lies under the facade.

My MOTHER HAD MOVED TO SANTE FE FOR SIX MONTHS FOR HER WORK. I WENT TO VISIT HER AND FELL IN LOVE WITH THE LIGHT, OPEN SMILES, SKIES, AND COLORS OF THE SOUTHWEST. I KNEW I WANTED TO MAKE THE SOUTHWEST MY HOME SOMEDAY.

HOW SHALL I STRUCTURE MY THOUGHTS?

NAD W/O ED

HOW NAKED BARE AND INSANELY, IMPULSIVELY CRAZY + VULNERABLE I FEEL W/O IT.

ART MUSIC HERE WE COME AND CACTUSES

TUCSON

Dining with friends | Noise in the Head

BUT RELIEF FROM THE
EATING DISORDER NEVER CAME.

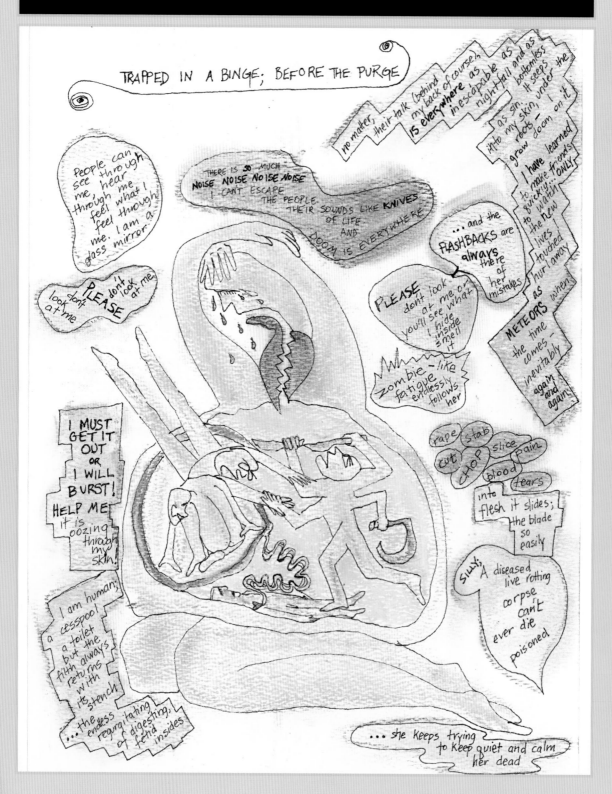

FEW STATES IN THE NATION HAVE ADEQUATE PROGRAMS OR SERVICES TO COMBAT EATING DISORDERS.

I BECAME MORE AND MORE HOPELESS.
I DIDN'T THINK I COULD EVER RECOVER.
I DIDN'T THINK I COULD LIVE.

I mean be
like a
sheep once
again off
to slaughter

I WAS PART OF A STUDY FOR THE TREATMENT OF DEPRESSION AND EATING DISORDERS. EVERY MONDAY, I WAS DISCUSSED AND PRESENTED TO THE TREATMENT TEAM.

THEY TRIED TO TEACH ME SELF-ESTEEM, TO CHANGE MY BEHAVIOR, TO CHANGE MY THINKING. THEY TRIED TO CHALLENGE MY NEGATIVE OBSESSIVE THOUGHTS ABOUT FOOD AND MY BODY.

LOOKING UP AT THOSE MEETINGS WAS THE HARDEST THING OF ALL.

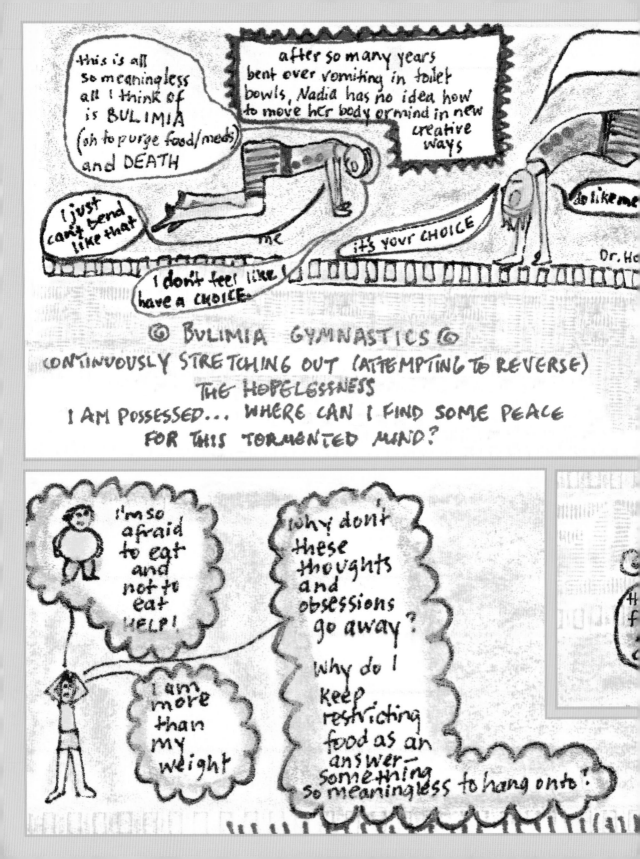

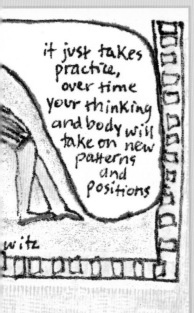

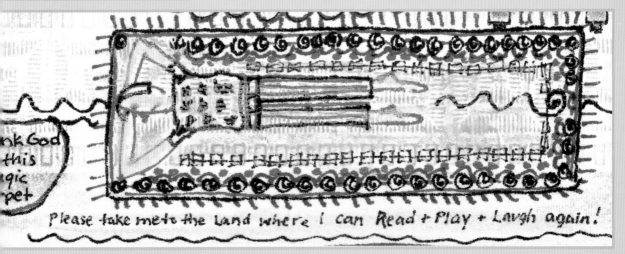

EATING DISORDERS REQUIRE A COMPREHENSIVE TREATMENT PLAN INVOLVING MEDICAL CARE AND MONITORING, PSYCHOSOCIAL INTERVENTIONS, NUTRITIONAL COUNSELING, AND, WHEN APPROPRIATE, MEDICATION MANAGEMENT.

I LEARNED
TO SHOP,
TO COOK,
TO PLAY.

I TRIED
TO LEARN
TO DREAM,
TO HOPE, AND
TO LAUGH.

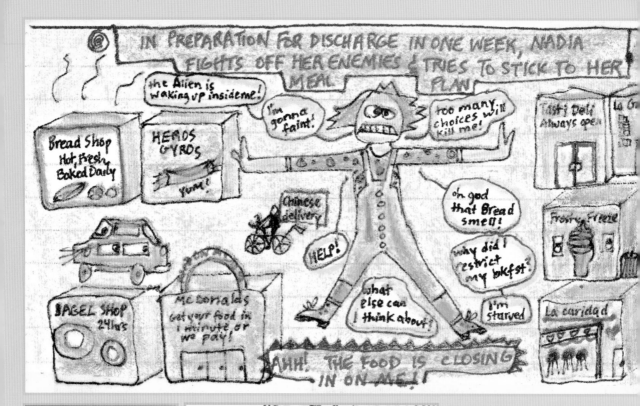

IT WAS SUCH HARD WORK. EVEN WITH ALL THIS SUPPORT I WAS SURE I WOULD FAIL.

FIFTY PERCENT OF THOSE SUFFERING FROM AN EATING DISORDER REPORT BEING CURED.

LUCKILY I WAS CAUGHT.

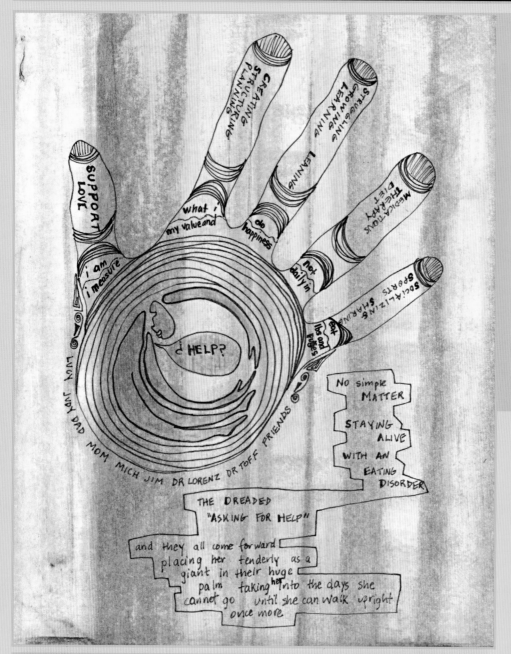

ABOUT SEVEN MILLION WOMEN AND ONE MILLION MEN SUFFER FROM EATING DISORDERS IN THE UNITED STATES.

I BEGAN TO COLLECT HOPE.

I'VE COME TO REALIZE, AFTER SO MANY SHARED EXPERIENCES WITH SO MANY WOMEN WHO SUFFER, THAT EACH ONE HAS HER OWN CREATIVE ROAD TO RECOVERY.

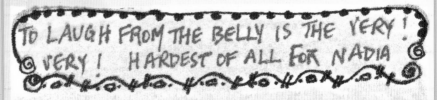

WITH TIME, I KNOW I'LL FIND MORE
MEANING AND LAUGHTER AND ACCEPTANCE
OF MY BODY. WITH TIME, I KNOW
THE ALIEN LYING IN THE EMPTINESS
INSIDE ME WILL SHRINK DOWN
TO THE SIZE OF A PEA.

THAT WILL BE GOOD ENOUGH FOR ME.

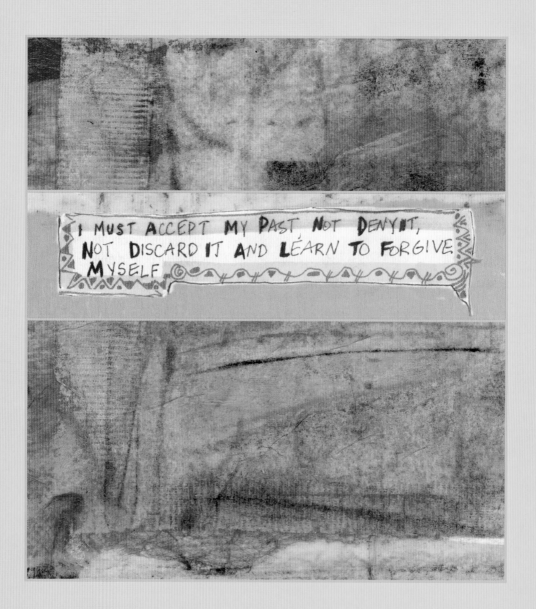

I MUST ACCEPT MY PAST, NOT DENY IT, NOT DISCARD IT AND LEARN TO FORGIVE MYSELF

AFTERWORD

I'VE BEEN HOSPITALIZED SEVERAL MORE TIMES
SINCE THIS BOOK WAS FIRST CONCEIVED AND
ILLUSTRATED. DAY BY DAY I CONTINUE
TO RECOVER, WORKING ON REPLACING
THE CRITICAL VOICE IN MY HEAD WITH ONE
THAT IS MORE POSITIVE AND LOVING.
I HOPE THAT BY READING THIS BOOK, WE WILL
INCREASE OUR UNDERSTANDING AND AWARENESS
OF EATING DISORDERS AND LESSEN THE SHAME,
GUILT, AND ISOLATION THAT SO OFTEN
OCCURS IN WOMEN SUFFERING FROM THEM,
WHICH KEEPS SO MANY WOMEN AND GIRLS
IN SILENCE AND MAKES THIS ILLNESS
SO HARD TO TREAT. THIS BOOK HAS BEEN
MY INSPIRATION TO CONTINUE TO RECOVER,
TO KNOW THAT I MIGHT, IN TIME, BE ABLE
TO REACH OUT TO OTHERS STILL SUFFERING.

If you, or someone you know, struggles with an eating disorder, you may find the following resources helpful. Please note that this list is provided only for reference, and that the author and publisher are not responsible in any way for the content of the websites for these sources.

National Eating Disorders Association
Provides resources and information about eating disorders
Website: www.nationaleatingdisorders.org
Tel.: (206) 382-3587
E-mail: info@nationaleatingdisorders.com

National Association of Anorexia Nervosa and Associated Disorders
Explores education, research, and facilities for treatment
Website: www.anad.org
Tel.: (847) 831-3438

Eating Disorders Anonymous
Offers information about local support groups
Website: www.eatingdisordersanonymous.org
E-mail: info@eatingdisordersanonymous.org

American Dietetic Association
Provides nutritional resources and information
Website: www.eatright.org
Tel.: (800) 877-1600

Eating Disorders Information Network
Offers educational information and treatment referrals
Website: www.edin-ga.org
Tel.: (404) 816-3346
E-mail: dina@edin-ga.org

MedLine Plus
A list of resources compiled by the U.S. National Library of Medicine and the National Institutes of Health
Website: www.nlm.nih.gov/medlineplus/eatingdisorders.html

Academy for Eating Disorders
Worldwide organization of professionals specializing in eating disorders; also provides information and referrals
Website: www.aedweb.org
Tel.: (847) 498-4274
E-mail: info@aedweb.org

Acknowledgments

I wish to extend my endless thanks to the treatment teams at New York Presbyterian and New York Cornell hospitals (inpatient, day treatment, and DBT programs), and the many professionals and treatment teams as well as fellow patients who extended their hands, hearts, and ears to me when I often had given up. I'd also like to thank all the mental health workers and aides who truly were there, often after hours and around the clock, when I most needed the comfort to go on. In Tucson, I would like to thank Community Partnership of Southern Arizona (CPSA), and the incredible individuals who created the Recovery Support Specialist (RSS) program. The hope it inspires is magic. Last but not least there are my doctor, my treatment team, and my family and friends who refused to give up on me. I couldn't have come this far without them. Special thanks to Susan Burke, who helped put this book together, and to Kristy Raffensberger, who was there to answer my questions. Most of all, I'd like to thank Bruce and Ginee, who first saw my sketches on napkins and kept after me to bring this project home.

FORTY-TWO PERCENT OF STUDENTS BETWEEN THE FIRST AND THIRD GRADES WANT TO BE THINNER.   —WWW.WOMENSISSUES.ABOUT.COM

EIGHTY PERCENT OF WOMEN ARE DISSATISFIED WITH THEIR APPEARANCE.   —WWW.WOMENSISSUES.ABOUT.COM

FORTY-FIVE PERCENT OF WOMEN ARE ON A DIET ON ANY GIVEN DAY.   —WWW.WOMENSISSUES.ABOUT.COM

WHEN THE PRESSURES OF ATHLETIC COMPETITION ARE ADDED TO AN EXISTING CULTURAL EMPHASIS
ON THINNESS, THE RISKS INCREASE FOR ATHLETES TO DEVELOP DISORDERED EATING.   —WWW.NATIONALEATINGDISORDERS.ORG

BULIMIA NERVOSA AFFECTS TWO OUT OF EVERY HUNDRED ADOLESCENT AND YOUNG ADULT WOMEN. —WWW.NATIONALEATINGDISORDERS.COM

IPECAC ABUSE CAN LEAD TO IRREGULAR HEARTBEAT, RAPID HEART RATE, CARDIAC ARREST, AND SUDDEN DEATH.   —WWW.ANAD.ORG

ONE-THIRD OF INDIVIDUALS WHO SUFFER FROM EATING DISORDERS REPORT THAT THE ONSET OF
THEIR ILLNESS OCCURRED BETWEEN THE AGES OF ELEVEN AND FIFTEEN.   —WWW.ANAD.ORG

EATING DISORDERS ARE NOT DUE TO A FAILURE OF WILL OR BEHAVIOR. THEY ARE REAL,
TREATABLE MEDICAL ILLNESSES IN WHICH CERTAIN PATTERNS OF EATING TAKE ON A LIFE OF THEIR OWN.   —WWW.NIMH.NIH.GOV

SIDE EFFECTS FROM PURGING INCLUDE: RUPTURE OF THE ESOPHAGUS, TOOTH DECAY, DEHYDRATION,
ELECTROLYTE IMBALANCES, IRREGULAR HEARTBEATS, POSSIBLE HEART FAILURE . . . AND DEATH.   —WWW.NATIONALEATINGDISORDERS.ORG

BULIMIA NERVOSA IS FREQUENTLY ASSOCIATED WITH SYMPTOMS OF DEPRESSION AND CHANGES
IN SOCIAL ADJUSTMENT.   —WWW.NATIONALEATINGDISORDERS.ORG

MANY PEOPLE STRUGGLING WITH BULIMIA NERVOSA RECOGNIZE THAT THEIR BEHAVIORS ARE
UNUSUAL, EVEN DANGEROUS.   —WWW.NATIONALEATINGDISORDERS.ORG

NINETEEN PERCENT OR MORE OF COLLEGE-AGE WOMEN IN AMERICA ARE BULIMIC.   —WWW.WOMENSISSUES.ABOUT.COM

THE SOONER EATING DISORDERS ARE DIAGNOSED AND TREATED, THE BETTER THE OUTCOMES ARE LIKELY TO BE.   —WWW.NIMH.NIH.GOV

ONLY A SMALL NUMBER OF SCHOOLS AND COLLEGES HAVE PROGRAMS TO EDUCATE YOUNG PEOPLE ABOUT THE
DANGERS OF EATING DISORDERS.   —WWW.ANAD.ORG

SOME MEDICATIONS, PRIMARILY ANTIDEPRESSANTS, HAVE BEEN FOUND HELPFUL FOR PEOPLE WITH BULIMIA,
PARTICULARLY THOSE WITH SIGNIFICANT SYMPTOMS OF DEPRESSION OR ANXIETY.   —WWW.NIMH.NIH.GOV

IN SPITE OF TREATMENT, TWENTY PERCENT OF PEOPLE WITH EATING DISORDERS MAKE ONLY PARTIAL RECOVERIES.
—WWW.WOMENSISSUES.ABOUT.COM

FEW STATES IN THE NATION HAVE ADEQUATE PROGRAMS OR SERVICES TO COMBAT EATING DISORDERS.   —WWW.ANAD.ORG

EATING DISORDERS REQUIRE A COMPREHENSIVE TREATMENT PLAN INVOLVING MEDICAL CARE AND MONITORING, PSYCHOSOCIAL
INTERVENTIONS, NUTRITIONAL COUNSELING, AND, WHEN APPROPRIATE, MEDICATION MANAGEMENT.   —WWW.NIMH.NIH.GOV

FIFTY PERCENT OF THOSE SUFFERING FROM AN EATING DISORDER REPORT BEING CURED.   —WWW.ANAD.ORG

ABOUT SEVEN MILLION WOMEN AND ONE MILLION MEN SUFFER FROM EATING DISORDERS IN THE UNITED STATES.   —WWW.ANAD.ORG

ALL SEGMENTS OF SOCIETY—MEN AND WOMEN, YOUNG AND OLD, RICH AND POOR, AND ALL RACES—ARE AFFECTED BY EATING DISORDERS.   —WWW.ANAD.ORG